Homage to Happiness

Homage to Happiness

Judith Krause

HAGIOS PRESS

Library and Archives Canada Cataloguing in Publication

Krause, Judith, author
Homage to happiness / Judith Krause.

Poems.
ISBN 978-1-926710-29-7 (pbk.)

I. Title.

PS8571.R386H65 2014 C811'.54 C2014-905516-1

Edited by Harold Rhenisch.
Designed and typeset by Donald Ward.
Cover art: *AC-87-119*, by William Perehudoff (1987), acrylic on canvas, 32" x 55". Used with the permission of Perehudoff Artwork. Hagios Press wishes to acknowledge the kind support of the Perehudoff family.
Cover design by Tania Wolk, Go Giraffe Go.
Set in Minion Pro.
Printed and bound in Canada at Houghton Boston Printers and Lithographers, Saskatoon.

The publishers gratefully acknowledge the assistance of the Saskatchewan Arts Board, The Canada Council for the Arts, and the Cultural Industries Development Fund (Saskatchewan Department of Culture, Youth & Recreation) in the production of this book.

Hagio Press
Box 33024 Cathedral PO
Regina SK S4T 7X2
www.hagiospress.com

For my family, especially Smith

I can wake up in the morning and I am happy.
Extraordinarily happy with no traceable cause.

— Agnes Martin, 1912–2004

Contents

Everything 12
Watching the Horses on Old Orchard Road 14
The Sounds of Happiness 15
Changes 16
I Wanted to See the World 17
Estrangement 18
Hen House 19
Footnotes to the Headlines 24
You Would Say 25
Up at Night 26
Wild Horses 28
Cathedral Village 29
  North of the Spires, South of the Tracks 29
  House Envy 30
  Henderson Terrace 31
  In the Heart of the Neighbourhood 33
Lines for the Romantic. . . . 35
Rules for Falling in Love 36
The Coat is a River 38
Homage to Happiness 39
  Painting 39
  My Birthplace 40
  Catatonia 41
  Coenties Slip 1957 42
  Good Car 43
  Cuba, New Mexico 45
  With My Back to the World 46
  Worth 47
  If I Could Tell You Anything 49
  In My Studio, Taos 1992 50
  Solo Exhibition 51
  The Perfection of the Morning 52

Purple Pitcher Plants 53
Everywhere the News 55
Six Degrees of Separation 56
Dipstick 59
Sixty 61
2013 62
Hourglass 63
Apology 65
Star Clock 66
Boundaries 68
Valentines 69
A Poet Walks into the Bar 71
Irving Layton in Regina 72
Contact Me 73
Ode to Discards 74
The Rites of Spring 76
Sunshower Flowering Tea 78
Little Buddha Man 80
Der Struwwelpeter 81
Village Laundry 83
Gender Reveal 85
Gingerbread 86
Chili Tomatoes 87
Things to Eat Before You Die 89
Mitterand's Last Meal 90
The Woman Who Swallowed History 91
Payload 93
My Sicily 94
Our Berlin 95
Your London 97
Her Paris 99
Dead or Alive 101
Black Dog Syndrome 102
The Snake Handler's Word of God 104

Wilf Perreault's *Guiding Light (2002)* as Sanctuary 105
The Heist 107
How to Reach the Sea 109

Acknowledgements 110

Homage to Happiness

Everything

. . . that vast/confused library, the female mind.
— Ruth Stone, *Male Gorillas*

Whatever you need is there,
tucked away somewhere in a fusty stack
or filed in a digital archive.

Confused? That doesn't begin to describe
the perplexities of a storage system
invented by silver-tongued scribes,

clay tablets stacked sky high, recounting
the Egyptian view of creation — all those omens
about the sun, the moon, thunder,

lightning, planets, and clouds. Who knew
how much the Greeks would end up
loving their word lists, their spellbinding

signs and symptoms, and medical diagnoses.
To say nothing of those who followed — the Romans
and Christians, among others, and now you.

But why worry so much? It's not as if a kiss
is some kind of trick. The brain
does indeed grasp the laws of attraction.

Besides, you aren't yet a living book, a text
no one will sign out, doomed
to languish in a private collection

until the final weeding out. You still
have dreams. You could even be
that Amazon librarian who straps on

a backpack and laces up knee high boots
to sprint to the bus stop at the end of the day,
a little out of breath as she settles into a seat,

hankering to lose herself in her book
for what would otherwise be
the humdrum ride home.

Watching the Horses on Old Orchard Road

A tall man folds himself —
long legs, long arms —
into a small neat package
almost disappearing
into the low green hedge
lining the roadside where
shadows embrace him.

Horses pastured in the old
orchard turn to watch
but only to be sure
he has nothing for them,
then swing their shiny rumps
to focus again on apples.

The man feels wind and sun
on his skin. He hears wasps
constant as buzz saws,
constant as the horses
gorging on windfalls.

How he loves the theater
of their rubber lips
twisting and lifting
over long yellow teeth,

a corral of sorts
for the impossibly
thick red tongues

they stick out as they work
and work every bit of sweetness

from the crisp fall air.

The Sounds of Happiness

We each have our own
— sex, champagne, work,
chocolate. . . . Simon's is
an hour-long antiphon
between a nightingale
and a bittern. Mine,
the rustle of prairie
chickens nestling
into a perfect brown
circle in my snowy
city yard on a bitter
January night.
Suzanne's, the ventriloquist
bird, nobody's fool,
who summers
in her crabapple tree.
Yours — fifty years
of no TV or radio and
no newspapers.

Changes

The wet years are the worst — water seeping
deep into soil and loosening the grip of earth.
The more the surface cracks, the longer the slide.
Sometimes whole sides of hills start to creep.
An inch here, a foot there. A tree falls. A boulder rolls.
You may not feel the shifting beneath your feet,
but the dog knows. He won't leave the field
far below in the valley where the toe of the slump
edges towards your farmhouse, lights flickering,
the sky darkened by yet another storm.

I Wanted to See the World

Maps hung on the wall over my childhood
bed with little pins marking all the places
my parents had visited. I too wanted to travel,
to ride trains at night, and wake up somewhere
I had never been, under a cloudless sky,
wanted to take the grand tour, spend
the year abroad, wander for a gap year,
live a year in England, a summer in the south
of France, part of some pre-ordained life
plan that takes no account of history or politics
or even desire, but my trip was ruined
in the end by weather, floods, and fire.
Then time ran out and wave after wave
swallowed everything in sight.

Estrangement

Cut grass and the sweet
sound of a horn — some song
I almost recognize but can't quite
put my finger on — draw
me from my quiet room out
into the bright fall air
and the armchair, carelessly parked
at the edge of the field,
where I sprawl,
noon sun on my face, alone

until you come along
to smoke, waving your white
plume through the air.
You comment on the spiders,
still as stoics: statuary
posed on the stones around us. Look,
you say, they must
be related. See how they all
face the same direction,
not moving a single limb
in the quickening wind.

Hen House

i

Mahogany hen sniffing anthyrium stem

This is the title of the image
on the birthday card
my sister sends —

happy she'll always be
younger and thinner,
and a natural blonde.

The colour of this
bird's plumage matches
my current dye job

though my hair is not
as glossy and thick.
It's hard to keep

secrets from someone
who knows my real
bra size and worst fears.

Old hens now, we can
only laugh since
we've pretty much

used up all we had
except our cackle
and crow.

ii

Rusty hen with key

We come home
once a week
to sort and clean.

The house holds
everything that belongs
to our mother —
the echo of her laugh,
the smell of her lotion,
the muddle of her mind.

A mess of papers everywhere.

By the end of the day
we are worn out
and cranky.

Each of us leaves
feeling like Henny Penny —
the one who did all the work.

iii

Chickens love tea

Who remembers when
chickens excelled
at motherhood, joining

their sisters in the nest box,
gathering their brood
under wing,

or teaching their chicks
how to bathe
in dust and peck for bugs?

In the days before
factory farms, a yolk
did not stick to its shell

because its mother
would turn her egg
at least fifty times a day.

In Ancient Rome, it was
a compliment to say
you had been raised by a hen.

Even so, any chicken
will gobble down an egg
— including her own.

iv

White black stick bird

Boxes of photographs fill
closet shelves and desk drawers.

The prints are black and white
with curled edges, snapshots

of people whose names
and faces we do not know.

None of us look like our mother.
She was a breed unto herself.

But we scramble like fierce old
biddies all over a June bug

to clutch one of her few
finished albums for ourselves.

v

Guinea fowl hurry along

Today we are looking
for our mother's will,

for the key
to her safety
deposit box,

for her good jewellery
and wedding ring.

So much gone forever.
So much still missing.

We fight our fear
the sky is falling.

No one says aloud:
You dumb cluck.
You bird brain.

Or where's your head?
Sayings we find
scratched by our mother

in her own shaky script
into a notebook
splayed on the counter.

Footnotes to the Headlines

Monarch butterflies are dying in record numbers —
their forests ravished. You confuse night and day.
Don't know the day of the week. Or the year.
Snowy owls are confused — airport runways are their new
landing strips. You get lost on your way home from
an oil change in the city where you lived your whole life.
Ten million beehives wiped out. The cause a mystery.
You lose your house key and wear the same
clothes for a week. Someone took your cane.
Left it outdoors in the hollyhocks that grow wild
between your house and the bungalow
next door. A young giraffe is slaughtered by its keepers,
then fed to lions during family visiting hours
at the zoo. You can't remember what you last ate.
Two months later, four of those lions are shot
to make room for a new male. You think your father is
still alive. You call your daughter by your mother's
name. Dolphins trapped by sharp Arctic ice
are filmed swimming in smaller and smaller
circles until they drown — the sea red
with their blood. You can't add. Can't spell.
You no longer know your own face in the mirror.
A Canadian cat breeder claims the Guinness World
Record for the fastest low-slung short cat
on the planet — you tell the same story every day
for a month. The punch line grows smaller
and smaller until all you have is a story without legs.

You Would Say

it was the moon tonight, the scent
of wanton night blooming flowers,
the way the delicate edges
of her gown billowed, all

smoke and flame, candle and wind,
how the stars stuck to their traditional
forms and the clouds moved away
with good grace and manners

and the dog's bone was buried
in soil so sweet, no one would know
what had happened. You would
say there is no need to speak again

and for many years I thought
you were right.

Up at Night

At any given time, somewhere
on one continent

or another, someone lies
awake in bed, chewing

over the grist of the day.
No warm milk.

No cool pillow
punched down and packed

under head will halt
the non-stop patter

of *Who said what to whom*
and in what tone,

or *Why did she make*
that face, you know the one —

I was sure you saw it too,
to *Is it the right time,*

and *How do I know?*
Worries pass from one

part of the mind to another
the way a cow plods

along the same worn path
from pasture to pasture,

oblivious to the open
gate that leads to

that wild green meadow
some call sleep.

Wild Horses

When my lover confides
something awful

is galloping through his body,
killing him,

I slam my fist on the table.
How can this be?

No man has moved
with greater grace.

When my lover says
his last words, months

before he takes his last breath,
months after the first

hint of what was to come,
the relentless

betrayal of muscle
and flesh, I can no

longer understand his speech,
think only of how his dark

eyes, untamed, hold everything
he needs me to know,

everything I wish
I could gentle, but can't.

Cathedral Village

i) *North of the Spires, South of the Tracks*

that's where my father's family finally moved,
in the early 50s, to the very edge of the West End,

the last house they would own,
the one that took them out of Germantown,

the one that meant no more boarders, though the basement floor
was dirt and they had to shovel coal to stay warm.

Early mornings, my grandmother, a devout convert, would walk
the eight blocks to the grand Catholic

cathedral with two spires and the enormous flight of stairs
that led straight to heaven. Were there bells before mass?

I can't recall. But there were other sounds — the constant
rumble of trains, their weight shaking the earth

and making the glasses in the kitchen cabinet rattle,
the sizzle, one summer, in the heat,

of an egg on the front walk,
and the slap of leaves in the tiny backyard

where mint and rhubarb grew and we cooled ourselves.
Occasionally, I was allowed to wander

down the back lane to the big barns
where milkmen housed their carts and draft horses. Sunday

was the only day we ever caught a glimpse of those
heavily-muscled animals standing docile

in their stalls. Every other day and night our corner
of the neighbourhood was full of the jingle of harnesses,

the clip clop of hooves and the smell of hay
and manure, cold comfort for my uncles

who never quit mourning the loss of the family
farm. The year my grandfather died, the dairy closed

the barn and my grandmother paved the backyard to
create an income for herself from five

parking spots rented to people who worked
in the big government offices downtown.

ii) *House Envy*

What Regina resident doesn't envy
the people who live in The Crescents,

one of the best old-house neighbourhoods
on the continent? Comfortably ensconced

in their timeless houses, our business class,
academia, up-and-comers and wannabes —

even my imaginary relatives in the mock
Queen Anne — can walk to downtown

offices on sidewalks sheltered by mature
trees. They can consider the public

park across the street a mere extension
of their own lush landscaping.

Notice that gracious sunroom over the garage.
Admire those stately leaded window mullions.

Who wouldn't want to be invited to a family meal
in one of these heritage homes, strolling up

the wide flagstone footpath to the great oak door
where the youngest is allowed to rap twice,

striking the brass lion on its shiny mane,
while we wait, under the gabled entrance,

for the master of the house to consider
whether he will admit us?

iii) *Henderson Terrace*

Like gangly bachelor uncles with bad teeth,
these tall red brick buildings
loom over the neighbourhood,

ghost ships from the past
marooned on the tiny
island of dirt between

Leopold Crescent and 18th Avenue.
The last examples of English
row housing in this flat prairie city,

they were built by an insurance king,
whose wife, of course, had her doubts.
Who'd want to live in such narrow

rooms with so many stairs? Well people did.
In 1913 and now. Her husband,
the great dreamer whose steady hand

drafted the construction plans, had a nose
for money. Was he smart enough
to sell off the property before claims

poured in that first wet spring
when the creek overflowed its banks?
Eight trendy condos stand guard

on low ground now, overlooking
the earthen dyke to the south
that was finally built in the 70s

to stave off floods in the small yards,
where, each June, peonies
and hardy lilacs, planted

almost a century ago, continue
to bloom. Their scent billows
on each fresh wave of air.

iv) *In the Heart of the Neighbourhood*

Who remembers the exotic
gift shop where we hung out
in the 70s and 80s whenever

we needed a fix of glamour,
the unusual, the odd,
some farrago, some salmagundi. . . .

whatever you wanted to call
that tangle, that welter
of goods gathered from all over

the globe and packed
into every corner of the main
floor of an old house

where the shopkeeper, a local
beauty with a past of some kind,
lived upstairs?

The moment you stepped across
that threshold, you entered
an emporium of the planet's

coolest toys, clothes,
trinkets, teas, and incense. Whenever
you needed a gift or March

slid into May or you decided
to skip class to rummage
through Indian bedspreads

and bright cotton tablecloths
looking for the perfect
orange, or to try on batik shirts

and long skirts for an hour,
was heavenly, a tonic for the soul.
What year did someone

decide to torch the store? The flames
spreading like a kitchen grease fire,
engulfing the neighboring homes

in the middle of the night?
It still seems sad, like love gone
wrong, to think a guy

would pour gasoline over the entrance
way, then light a match and step
back onto the curb,

glassy-eyed, sweating, to watch
until the scream of sirens
pumped enough

oxygen into his blood
that he could run.

Lines for the Romantic Who Lives Over the Hardware Store on Main Street

Tell me who, in this small town, didn't know
the man upstairs wept all night.

Tell me who hadn't heard his plaintive
song under our sole street light.

Everyone knew, each spring, a new couple
would imagine their future bright.

Everyone knew, below the bare
branches, they held each other tight.

And everyone knew why that man swept
and swept those whitewashed stairs.

Rules for Falling in Love

There are no rules.

No one tells your heart
to beat faster.

No one controls
your breath,

or that sudden flush —
heat coursing

through your veins —
a telltale sign

you will test positive
for this drug.

There should be a law
to regulate its use.

And to guard against
the inevitable

periods of sadness
and sorrow

when the chemicals
lose their power

to affect you.
Crosses and breaks

in your heartline
are normal.

You will recover.
Now tell me

the story of
how you met.

The Coat is a River

Sarah Hannah, "Self-Portrait in a Cocked Hat"

The coat is a river, the hat
a dark mountain

underneath, a landscape
not yet known,

her scarf, the wind.

She stands tall, runs
chapped hands
through long, wavy hair.

Have all the explorers
gone home for the day?

The bus is late, the train too….

when will she find
her way? Who can
she ask who knows

where to start, how
long to stay, where
to call it the end?

Homage to Happiness

Painting

This is what I was born to do.
Lines

are what I learned
in my early years
on the prairies, watching

the long freight trains
move for what seemed
like hours across the horizon

and the endless fields go
green gold brown white,
green gold brown white.

In my heart I know
the sound of the wind,
and the feel of blood

pushing to get to where
everything that matters
happens. After all,

we were always meant
to be verbs.

My Birthplace

At the junction
of Highways 31 and 14,

a horse ankle bone
98 times the size

of the real thing
lights the night sky.

From a distance, the town
emits an orange glow

that a stranger might
think radioactive

if he or she did not know
this is Macklin,

Saskatchewan, and the game
of bunnock is its claim to fame.

I left before I was old
enough to be taught how

to heave a Schmeiser
with sufficient force

to knock down a rival.
No matter. I mastered

a different game —
learning to draw

my eye over the level
ground of canvas,

where I played
as hard as I could

against myself,
each success celebrated

with a faint smile,
my feet planted

squarely on
my own terrain.

Catatonia

Sounds like a country
but it's the state

I visited on occasion
throughout my long life,

peopled with silence,
its citizens stone still.

On a round-the-world
voyage once, I had

to be taken off
the freighter in Bombay

and kept for a month
in hospital. My trances?

Periods of intense concentration.
Family worried they were

signs of psychotic disturbance.
Clinical in nature. Not the mark

of a deeply spiritual being
who could divorce

the world on a dime
any time I wanted to.

Coenties Slip 1957

The image is small, grainy.
A group of five or six of us

on a rooftop at dusk.
In spite of the bold caption

which points me out
sitting on the far right,

along with my now renowned
companions — Indiana,

and Kelly, Rosenquist,
Tawney and Wilson, it is

the unnamed child
who captures your eye.

What did that boy make
of this social occasion,

surrounded by some
of the greats in modern art?

Was it simply time
with Dad and his friends

overlooking the city
on a hot New York night?

Hard to say. Back then,
none of us knew

who would make it
and not one of us cared.

Good Car

A good car counted.
I knew how to look

after one, change
the oil and tires,

how to grease and polish
and give the engine a hard

test run — all
part of being able to take

care of myself. I needed
those skills in the years

I moved around
the continent, travelling

from one wild part of it
to another, keeping

company only with
animals who slept

as soundly as I did
at night.

Cuba, New Mexico

This is where
I chose to build

my new home,
by hand, by myself.

A place whose name
contains two countries:

my own, adopted,
and the other one

where people struggled,
the way perhaps

all immigrants struggle
to maintain their ties,

or milk the honey,
yet avoid the bee.

I finally had a studio,
but it was seven years

before my hand could
lift a brush again.

With My Back to the World

I have no ideas of my own.
I empty my mind every day

and wait for inspiration.
Alone, my back to the world,

I seek the sublime.
Nothing in nature

can match the happiness
I find in rectangles —

so much friendlier
and welcoming than squares.

The grid is my door
to the universe.

Bands of colour wash
through me onto the canvas —

green waves of beauty.

Worth

Think of the man in Saskatoon
who spotted a small

canvas in a spring
yard sale, and was struck

by something, some hint
of the universe, then moved

to shell out ten
or twenty bucks to take it home,

and who then learned
this glimpse of the world,

witnessed in travels
in the early days of my career,

is worth considerably
more than his home.

That's what's wrong
with the art market.

That's why my agent
has been instructed

to donate every
painting I now make

to an underfunded
public collection. If I could,

I would house all my work outdoors
under the unfixed sky

where there'd be a chance,
slight, perhaps, I know,

that you could see
what I do.

If I Could Tell You Anything

I would tell you
you have time

as long as you do not
live in the middle

class world or have
children or pets or a

regular job. Do not watch
TV or read papers.

You have time as long
as you never let

anyone into your studio
or your mind

or worry about what others think
you ought to be doing.

Remember your work
is your work.

It is not mine.
And you do have time.

In my Studio, Taos 1992

At 80, I gaze
straight into the camera.

From the look in my eyes,
you would never say

I am lost
in the moment.

My graying hair is parted
(no fuss, no nonsense)

on the side, my large hands
at ease, hanging over

the ends of the armrests, as exotic
as two bunches of bananas.

The stiff white collar
on my dark shirt sets off

the ruddiness of my cheeks
and the firm line of my mouth.

You can't guess
what I am thinking

but it's clear my mind
occupies every inch

of the stark
space around me.

Solo Exhibition

At last, I have found my way
to the centre, to that place

on the canvas where every
detail, every brush stroke,

counts.
There is no need for speech.

I know the subtleties
of clear bright light. I know

the draw of clean air.
This is why we cross

a deserted beach
to stare at the ocean

or why we sit for hours
on the top of a hill

with the wind in our hair.
There are only two directions:

in and out.
I paint

in the space
where the sacred is contained,

that distance between perfection
and my very human hand.

The Perfection of the Day

Six feet by six feet. This is
the painting in your dream.

I am standing there,
looking,

reading the line of earth and sky,
my grid,

a kind of geometry
of breath — of air.

There is algebra too.
When the clouds

and the wind
perform their daily

rite of complex
calculations, you could say

they were equations,
you could say

they were songs
the grass is singing.

Purple Pitcher Plants

i

Hard to fathom why the world's only cold climate carnivorous
plant was chosen to represent Newfoundland and Labrador.

After all, what does this say about the place and its people?
Beware of the deep? Things aren't quite as they seem? Of course,

the population's already sparse and the land rough and barren.
Any flower that manages to thrive on that poor soil is a marvel —

life humming at the bottom of its long narrow throat
at the spot where water collects, tricking

its prey — ants, spiders, flies — into taking one tiny
sip before the grand finale

ii

Across the great pond, trust the English to go one further.
Like Nigel, the Somerset nurseryman, who is staggered

when he discovers in his tropical garden one of his pitcher
plants has eaten a bird, a blue tit, no less,

(Note: not a coal tit or a marsh tit or a great tit but a blue one)
that, he theorizes, must have tipped

too far in its reach for an insect floating on
the pool of water at the base of the flower, then

drowned. All that shows now — tail feathers and a few
tufts of wings — makes a sticky cross, of sorts.

iii

One of my neighbours, born overseas in the 50s to a Canadian
soldier on a military base, claims she is a Newfie, though

she's lived 30 of her 34 years of adult
life on the prairies. Her young father, desperate

to find a way to support a new bride and their dreams
of a family, ended up at the front of the line in the recruiting

office on April 1, 1949, the day after their beloved
dominion became a province of Canada, something

his own father never let him forget — that his only son, that boob
of a boy, was the first fool

from the colony to sign up — a fact that festered
in the old man's craw till the day his death kit was laid out.

Everywhere the News

The armless man who head butts his rival to death.

The long overdue formal apology to 80,000 First
Peoples wounded by government decree.

The woman who loses everything after her
tubes are tied into a knot so tight it cuts
her circulation and her arms and legs need
to be cut off, and her mind retreats
to the time she was seven,
one year older than her oldest child.

The uncle who mouths on his deathbed
that he's stopped drinking
for good this time.

Golden apple-shaped pears ripen on a tree
hanging over an electric fence, easy
pickings for the horses, not
for us. The fruit also loved by a bee so big with a bite so bad
we are warned we'd rather be
kicked in the gut than stung.

The handyman who can fix everything
tells me the cows were bawling
all night long for their young
just sent to market. He says nothing will make them stop
but time.

Six Degrees of Separation

Bill, the fashion guy
whose commentary
appears each week
on a New York Times website
telling us who's wearing what
on the big city streets
in a voice so much
like my friend Dave's,
I am always startled
when I hear Bill go on
about the wonders of leggy
women in high heels,
and how marvelous
the little dogs were this year,
dressed to the nines
in tartans and plaids
at the Easter parade,
and how people on the avenue
look terrific this spring
in their casually belted
short khaki trench coats
with raglan sleeves
and big tortoise shell buttons.

Bill has an impeccable eye
for line and seams.
He knows gloves,
collars and hoods, and is crazy
about fringe. He loves
pinstripes, and cuffs
and a good show of thigh.
He loves the way
women in the city

adore black all
season long, how colour
repeats itself
and the fact fashions return,
though never the same.
He knows the old ideas are gone
but revels that the imagination
reigns supreme.
Bill is a style hound,
riding his bike everywhere,
watching what people
are wearing, sniffing
out trends before
anyone even knows they're here.

If Bill ever saw
his voice twin, Dave,
he'd be hard pressed to name
Dave's fashion style. Never mind
that neither one actually
comes from where they sound
like they come from.
Bill would say Dave stretches
a very long arm back
into a 60s-era closet
where comfort in the form
of faded jeans and flannel shirts
with rolled up sleeves created
a kind of uniform
worn by an entire
generation. Dave might tell Bill
to fuck off, but in a gentle
voice, given their
apparently shared vocal genetics.

Unlike most twins
separated at birth, these two
would find they have little
in common, then laugh
their long low chuckles,
indistinguishable.

Dipstick

Wood Islands, PEI

How could Chris and Mary, a MacDonald
and a MacLeod, not know it was dangerous
to let their dogs swim out into the strait
just past where the ferry docks. Didn't they
walk their dogs along that private beach
at the same time nearly every day? Hadn't Chris,
the lobster fisherman, remarked to Mary
many times of late that seals in the area
were becoming more aggressive, stealing
bait right out of his traps? When did the couple
realize seven or eight of those dog-faced
mammals had surrounded their favorite
Lab mix? A quarter mile out,
with the tide coming in, what did Dippy think
of the sleek coal-gray animals nudging her,
at first in play, and then nibbling at her paws?
By then, no amount of calling, yelling
or screaming helped. Chris watched,
as Mary, the stronger swimmer, swam out as far
as she could, but the seals kept pushing the dog
further and further from shore until
the owners couldn't see her any more.

Featherheads, ninnyhammers, nitwits.
hard not to say, despite the heartbreak of their loss,
that the dog was aptly named for its owners,
but wait, maybe there's something more
going on here than a mere story
about a dog drowned by seals. Something no mooncalf,
numbskull or dolt should ignore. Perhaps
Chris had been crooning some strange

sorrowful song. Perhaps it was Mary,
a shapeshifter, unable to find her selkie
skin and return to her home in the sea. Or maybe the seals
were simply tired of the sound of human voices,
tired of smooth silvery human skin,
determined to explore life as a different
kind of creature, with fur.

Sixty

Another country,
another city, another house.
Most of your life behind you,
the future unknown.
Why make predictions
about how things will turn out.
You will be wrong
even if you get it
right, whether the end
is just around that unmarked
turn or lying
decades away under
tightly tucked sheets
in a single bed,
the dim light hard
on everyone's eyes,
the best china long gone,
the silver pawned.
Rest easy. No one can
steal your regrets, your small
sorrows, or your
conviction. Nothing, save
love, lies ahead.

2013

Lucky or unlucky, only you
can say if thirteen, the smallest
number with eight letters, triggers

that terror of twelve-plus-one
which can decimate you anywhere —
at the bank, the dinner table,

or in an elevator. No way to escape.
No way to not notice the missing
floor, the lost digits on hotel room doors.

To pretend you don't know thirteen
witches make a coven. Or refuse to give birth
in a month with two full moons.

Others believe thirteen is good
fortune, count aloud, as if in prayer,
each of the thirteen steps on the fabled

ladder to eternity, finger the thirteen
stripes on the American flag, even hope
to turn over the thirteenth tarot card

where Death, on his horse, is eager
for transformation. They do not understand
how anyone could be afraid of a number

only divisible by itself, a number that represents
the very age at which you, yourself, might be lucky
enough to become a man, or a woman.

Hourglass

As if that bandy-legged French
monk, Liutprand, wobbling

on his old sea legs up and down
the stone floors in the first

cathedral to be built on sacred
ground at Chartres, fully

understood how his little
invention would add to the instruments

anyone could use to measure
the elements of a life —

how long a breath, a meal, a trip,
a prayer — his flow of sand

more accurate than a slosh of water
in a glass bulb and more reliable

for plotting the journey home.
Even the poor young ship's page whose

job it was, centuries later, on Magellan's
trip around the globe, to turn over,

and over, the eighteen
hourglasses needed for navigation,

at different intervals — either
15, 30, 45 or 60 minutes — and then record

the times in the ship's log, or risk
a watery tomb, thanked God

daily for this equipment.
But what then of the sun,

the moon, the stars, shadows,
candles and incense sticks?

All the old ways. The lines
and circles of our lives.

Though the body only moves
in one direction, cradle to grave,

the mind keeps its own time,
travelling from the future

to the past,
and back again.

Apology

Bluetailed skink on the wall
forgive me, first of all,
for calling you by the wrong name.
I did so rightly admire
your iridescence as you stretched
your long slim body along
the line of noonday sun
on the garden path.
Trust me, later
I noted the quick
flick of your disposable
tail, that deft defense against
enemies, when you sped
across my bathroom
floor. I am sorry
I have no trick quite
as charming
to disarm
my own foes.

Star Clock

Santa Fe, New Mexico

Under the dark
desert sky, I see the tail
end of the constellation
of my childhood,

the little twinkle
twinkle of the largest
cub following its two
siblings and fierce mama.

My own mother lives far
to the north of me
where her fate is sealed
by the total mass of her history

rapidly burning now
at the end of its time.
Even though it's said no
tools are needed to

determine the hour
of night or day, only simple
addition and quick subtraction,
tonight I cannot accurately

measure the position
of the Big Dipper. I do not know
which part of the hemisphere to use
as a baseline. All the star

charts glow with the luminosity
of our separate lives:
massive balls of plasma,
held together by the gravity of time.

Boundaries

A thousand light years
away, in the constellation Perseus,
astronomers have detected
a colony of strange objects
that straddle the boundary
between planets and stars.

Identified as brown dwarfs,
they are the smallest and coldest
light-throwing bodies
in the universe.
In your mother's secret
bureau drawer,

months after her
death, you find
a bundle of letters neatly
tied together. The ink is brown.
The paper is brown.
And you are torn.

Do you want to know
the contents or toss out
some of her history unread?
Even the light from a failed
star is bright enough
to ruin your sleep.

Valentines

At last Cupid is here.
It's nearly midnight and he's on

the front step, ringing the bell,
and dancing from foot

to foot in the bitter cold,
slapping his beefy arms, his

own private bear hug.
Through the peephole, he seems

to be mouthing juicy
wee love bites

but it's hard to know for sure.
I let him cool some in the frosty air.

My neighbors would love me
to tell my men not to

drive up and down our street after dark
with only their parking lights on

but they are afraid, crazy
old lady that I am,

I might get mad
and give out their address instead

while the little girl next door
will chatter now for weeks

to everyone in earshot about how
she massacred the other girls

in Grade Two. Her haul of hearts
broke all the records.

The truth is, her mother confides,
Molly was the only child

in her class who did not receive
a single valentine.

A Poet Walks into the Bar

Humor is the instinct for taking pain playfully
— Max Eastman

Did you hear the one
the poet told us,

how every poem
is built like a joke —

clean jokes, fat jokes,
blonde jokes, kids jokes —

it doesn't matter.
If you want to become

a funny person, say
the life of the party,

you must learn
how to lighten

moods, how to tell a good
joke from a bad one,

how to read an audience,
how to deliver lines,

how to know if a dirty
joke will fly,

or die. It all comes
down to the secrets

of telling — avoid
unnecessary detours.

Irving Layton in Regina

And the Word was made flesh, and dwelt among us.
— John 14:1

The first time Irving
Layton stopped in Regina,
in the early 70s on a national
book tour a few curious people
braved a late spring
blizzard to wait, without complaint
in those uncomfortable
seats in the old Darke Hall,
for the reading
to start. The small
stage was occupied by a cleaner
with silvery shoulder-length hair
who swept dust off the grand
piano with long sleeves,
twirled three times on the stool,
then strutted up to the mic,
a large bronze medallion,
centered on his sizeable
turtle-necked chest, to boldly
utter the first of what became
scores of ardent lyrics
igniting that cold night.

Contact Me

In the hierarchy of authors
who attract reader response,
poets come in last.

No one writes to correct the facts or ask
for more examples. No one questions
the source of a line or image.

Biographers and essayists,
even novelists and memoirists,
court closer attention. What is it

about a form that creates
fans so ready to
silence their own tongues?

Ode to Discards

Here's to the unwanted,
the castoffs, the leftovers,
what remains when the first
round has been chosen,
and my gift,
five writing prompts that did not speak
to a poet friend, calls out hey,
make something, if you can, of us,
and so I do,
reclaiming the faded denim of my mother's eyes
for the first, my blue
object, then smelling that odd summer
shower mix of dust
and rain on a gravel road, as my second,
where the wind relentlessly rustles the aspen,
my third, and the furnace of the sun
heats my skin like the interior
heater in my first car,
a '73 VW Super Beetle,
the fourth, that ran, season in, season out,
scorching bare ankles
or barely warming winter boots in that dark
arctic time of the year when you can hardly
remember how your tongue,
only six months earlier, burst
the first plump Saskatoon berry,
your favorite food,
the fifth, against your teeth,
staining everything
purple, berries so ripe they practically
fall from the branches
into your pail, so many at once,
some hitting the ground,

where they will be
redeemed, much later, by the many
small and grateful
animals of night.

The Rites of Spring

In your childhood home, everyone had a hand
in science projects. A visitor might find a nail

rusting away in a recapped bottle of Coke or
a dried hen's head hanging on a hook

at the back door — no evidence of teeth after all.
Someone was always trying to grow penicillin

or build a vinegar volcano or prove that
raisins dance in a bottle of clear soda.

Five boys and a dad who'd never wanted
to grow up. How did your mother stand it?

At the first sign of spring, all of you emptied
dresser drawers of socks, plucking those without

mates from under beds or out of boots.
Your dad in the lead, you paraded down to the dock

to stand at the shore (the ice on the lake still melting,
the wind raw) and built a roaring bonfire of woolens,

cottons and the rare synthetic. From then till freeze up,
every hot-blooded Johnson male sported bare feet.

Today, in the clean and tidy home you share
with wife and daughters, you are alone

in your desire for experiments.
Your children find you funny,

amusing, a little odd, your wife, endearing.
Tonight, in honour of the equinox,

this seasonal tipping point between night and day,
you will set a dozen

raw eggs upright on the kitchen counter
and in the morning, when you count how many

kept their balance on their round white
ends, you will call your closest brother

to see how many stood up at his place,
your voice high pitched, your words

racing over the phone line, down the street
and through the back lane

to where he lives, both of you
incredulous, awestruck, boys again.

Sunshower Flowering Tea

The glass teapot shimmers
in the morning sun. Steam,

collecting in the lid, forms
large drops that fall,

slow motion, into hot
water, where,

before our widening eyes,
a small dark

bud gives birth to
an entire spring garden.

One minute, slender green
shoots unfold.

Then bubbles shoot up.
Bits and pieces of life

float to the top. A final
burst of bright

colour and we are
stunned by the arrival of fragrance —

jasmine, lily, chrysanthemum —
exotic perfumes from

lands halfway around the world.
Ancient art or modern

miracle, who cares?
The legend of each tea's

origin might be the stuff
of some marketing

man's dream but somewhere
someone on this

planet learned the art
of folding and sewing

long damp leaves into hand-tied
balls that hold us still

for the time it takes
to be reborn.

Little Buddha Man

for S.J.K.

For many weeks you rest,
head under your mother's ribs,
one hand holding up your thoughts,
the other waving them away.
When her waters break, it is time
to leave one world for another,
though you are in no hurry,
cross legged and comfortable
on the throne of her hips, your face
calm and skin golden. You know
what you think is what
you will become. Your mouth
opens to taste the hospital air,
your lungs fill, then empty,
and suddenly the room is not quite
big enough to hold you.

Der Struwwelpeter

Oh Peter, slovenly one,
the true story of your birth
is a classic tale of a father's love for his son,
a frantic father unable to find
the perfect gift for his young boy,
so that he, Herr Hoffmann, felt
forced to create you, late at night,
hunched over a table, working by candlelight,
delivering you just in time for Christmas
1845, in a handmade book,
Heinrich's idea of cheerful stories
and comic drawings for good little folks.
Peter, you need to know you were a hit,
in spite of your poor grooming,
popular with parents and children alike,
appearing soon after your birth
in editions all over Europe. Everyone
relished the pretty stories and funny pictures,
and the clear moral message:
misbehavior equals disaster.
Your childhood companions —
Johnny Look-in-the-Air, Fidgety Philip,
Sophie Spoil-all, and Envious Minny —
couldn't keep up to the antics
of Idle Fritz, Heedless Hugo, Prying Will
and Ned the Toy Breaker.
But the worst were Simple
Hans and Cruel Paul. Such a relief
when you finally took up with Slovenly Betsy.

All of you, of course, scared to death
of Doctor Wango Tango
and his thin horse Sam. Today you live on
in so many versions of childhood truth,
it is a wonder you weren't banned.
Every Little Suck-a-Thumb I know
still dreads the tall, dark, Scissorman.

Village Laundry

Birkenau, Autumn 1941

Something is spoiled. But what?
Feliks doesn't understand
why his mother looks so small
and glum when she hangs the wash
on the clothesline that divides
their narrow balcony

or why the neighbors grumble
about the smell that wafts
non stop down the tracks into town.
All day his mother frowns
and his mother scowls
and the sooty dust collects

on every pillow, on every sheet
and in every crease of every once
pure white quilt. Even feathers
have lost their loft and flight.
His grandfather says to ignore
the constant shudder

of the trains, the relentless
stench that rises
from the nearby stacks.
His grandmother insists
he wears his good gold cross
weekdays, not just for Sunday mass.

He doesn’t know where Aaron
or Jakob went. The teacher says
they may have gone to visit
family far away, so Feliks,
mind your own business,
and do your math.

Even the village busybody,
the seamstress who knows the size
and secrets of every local woman,
who waves her flashy bracelet of pins
to clear the foul air,
tells his mother she can’t figure out

what those Germans are growing
at the experimental farms
across the road where the freights
pull in day and night. Son,
his mother chides, it is time
for bed. Pay no attention

to the cruel way the wind bawls
through the now leafless birch —
I will sing you a lullaby.
Felix does not reply.
It is too late. No song he hears
can still his newborn fear.

Gender Reveal

for D.S.

Twenty weeks is the current ideal
time to see if you can see
what you will be having. But still
best to keep your receipts
in case the ultrasound technician misreads
those shadowy moving parts.

You can't just ask a shy child
to open his or her legs, or chide
the one who rides
the umbilical cord like a horse,
or be mad at the one loves to nestle,
hands cupped over the "goods."

But, at twenty years it's a different
story. No one in the family wants
to hear because everyone already knows
from those early days of dress-up and
Mom's underwear to the more recent fights
with Dad and bullying at school.

For the first coming out, some families hold
elaborate parties with pink or blue fillings
buried inside innocuous white cupcakes,
cameras poised to capture the moment
your bite reveals a son or daughter.
For the second, no surprise, and no more tears.

Gingerbread

I am searching for the timeless
cookie, the lost recipe, my mother's,

your mother's, that heavenly blend
of ginger, molasses and butter

baked into some sugared shape,
a little test cake for you to hold

under your nose, eyes closed,
deep breath in and out,

before you take the first bite.
With each new batch, I watch

how tenderly your mouth moves
as you chew, loss and pleasure

rolling over your tongue, watch
you check the roof of your mouth

for orphan morsels, smack
your well-licked lips together,

then wait to see if you will reach
across the table for my hand

to whisk us away, once again, and
forevermore, from the witch's house.

Chili Tomatoes

for Al

Help yourself, says the note
in the lunchroom, to what
my so-called tomato plants produced.
A large white platter holds
an elegant array of long glossy
chilies looking every bit like
a red version of green snap beans,
say Red Swan or Dragon's Tongue.
No one knows for sure
what kind of peppers these are
or how hot they will be,
but I take a few home, eager to test my limits
for raising the temperature
to the point where pleasure and pain
meet and peppers rule,
affirming perhaps that Yale
psychologist's definition of humans —
we are the only animals who like Tabasco sauce.
Other mammals know better
than to bite into a jalapeno
or mouth a ripe habanera.
Even two-percent capsaicin
is enough to keep a bear away.
Gotta love those grocery shelves
jammed with bottles of Frank's Hot Sauce,
Mad Dog Inferno and Scorned Woman,
wedged next to Ring of Fire,
Da' Bomb or Dat'l Do It Devil Drops.

The old Scoville method of rating
extreme heat now a selling feature
for sauces so hot they come with their own death
certificates and coffins. But tell that to
the father of a young British chef
who was found dead the morning after
eating a salsa made from chilies
from the family garden.

Things to Eat Before You Die

for dee

First of all, whittle the list,
leave off any food so dangerous
you'd have to have a death wish
to even want to eat it — the poisonous
puffer fish that only licensed handlers
in Japan dare prepare, the Sicilian cheese
so rotten maggots are used to age it,
the fermented Colombian homebrew
made with maize and human spit.
Why not decide, instead, to simply
eat your view? Who needs deep-fried
Mars bars when you can dine
on your own landscape? Where grains
and pulses package up a prairie summer,
and you can taste the sky and wind
and long days of sun on open fields.
Where the white and tender flesh of walleye
from cold northern lakes can make you
moan for more. Where, in the bush,
rains come at just the right time
to give the Saskatoons a silvery cast
and, with each spoonful of cloud,
you can't stop releasing bantam
bleats of unspoiled pleasure.

Mitterand's Last Meal

At last it is illegal to trap the ortolan,
those fragile songbirds the size of a small girl's fist
once so common in southwestern France.
Illegal now to poke out their eyes and keep the birds
in the dark, force feeding them millet
until their tiny frames swell to four times their size
and they are drowned in Armagnac.

Rumoured to be tastier than foie gras,
these buntings, roasted whole and plucked,
become two-ounce gourmand snacks,
a banned gastronomic feast
even a dying French president can't resist,
indulging, again, and for the last time, his
sensual nature and the pleasures of the table.

The ritual napkin over his head, the better to absorb
the maximum odour and flavours (and perhaps hide
the whole messy business from sight), an entire
bird is popped, back end first, into his dying mouth.
The beak, protruding ever so slightly
from his lips, is severed, then discarded,

as he chews and sucks and swallows
the sizzling yellow fat, the blood, the guts,
chewing and chewing until the small
roasted delicate bones that taste like hazelnuts
begin to cut into his gums and blood oozes
from the corners of his sated lips.

The Woman Who Swallowed History

It took almost seven decades for the woman
who swallowed history to break

her silence, for the *Sturm und Drang*
of what had happened to her

to erupt, the way a piece of shrapnel
might finally work itself free,

and for her secret, enshrined in layers
and layers of guilt, lies and shame,

to take on the translucent lustre of a pearl,
something of value she thinks

she will bequeath to a dutiful niece,
an inheritance of bald truth

on no occasion did she consider sharing
with her husband when he was alive.

But now she is once more a prisoner,
too frail and ill to leave the Berlin flat

in which she was born and where
she will soon die, a fact which liberates her

to reveal her wartime role as a young
and beautiful food taster for Hitler

and an incorrigible flirt with his guards
at Wolfschanze near the eastern border

where she never saw Der Führer in person
but played with his dogs, Blondi and Bella,

and where she was so well fed on rich dishes
spiked with the fear of poison

while others starved, she could not savour
spring asparagus in cream sauce

or the woodsy flavor of forest morels
or later forget that her life had been saved

by a whispered warning from an SS friend
to go back to devastated Berlin

only days before the rest of the kitchen staff
were shot to death, and where

in the first months after the war,
the Red Army so loved her well-padded

and plump figure, they treated her
to savage beatings and weeks of rape,

forcing her again and again
to swallow their rage and her shame,

killing any appetite she might
ever have for a normal life,

which is why she never bore children
or carried an extra ounce of weight.

Payload

Per ardua ad astra

i

Through adversity, through everything life threw at him,
he was an even-tempered, no-fuss funny guy
who never asked for much, except, at the end,
when he confided he'd always wanted to travel
into outer space and could she please arrange
for him to be shot into the cosmos, which actually
wasn't as hard to organize as it sounds, though only
a teaspoonful of his ashes would end up in transport
in a silver case about the size of a tube of her lipstick.

ii

To the stars, his presence means nothing. To her,
every eighty minutes when he passes over her house,
making his rounds through the heavens the way he used to walk
from room to room turning out lights, she thinks about
him. Some days she runs to the computer to track
his orbit — now over the South China Sea, now the Atlantic.
Some nights she watches the video of his launch.
Cloudless nights, she steps out into the backyard and follows,
with her naked eye, their last gift to each other.

My Sicily

That summer of intense heat
we drove at night with the windows down
until we reached the coastline.
You were almost home.
The ferry would be there
to greet us at dawn.

While we waited, you sang, you danced.
Your excitement was contagious.
How could your family
not love me too. The view
of Mount Etna in the distance
surreal in the silvery night.

Of course, things were
not as they seemed. I recall
the smell of garlic on your breath,
lemon zest under your nails,
and how your mother
never once smiled.

Years later, I read you died
unexpectedly, at home,
in the night, in the arms
of your lover, your wife
of twenty years, and did the math.
You liar, you cheat.

Our Berlin

How naïve, how little
we understood of the politics

of intimacy, how a great
city might be broken

and re-broken many times
through its long history,

how two longtime lovers
might bust up a union

so seemingly solid,
only a wall of stone blocks

erected from one end to the other
could divide its heart.

In hindsight, the things
we loved, the island of

museums by the river Spree,
the cathedral and tree-lined

streets were not loved enough
for what they were.

When the man we still hold
culpable for severing

the capital, that hardheaded
boorish leader of the Cold War,

Khrushchev, boasted
in a speech to Yugoslavs

in 1963 that Berlin was
the testicle of the West,

he didn't need to squeeze
his thick fingers to make his point.

Your London

City-boy slick, always changing, always
the same, impossible to know —

that's your London with all its odd
corners and shifting moods,

its charms so alluring, you knew
from your first-ever visit

on one of those rare childhood
father-son holidays, you could never

see enough of it. This photo is proof
of how smitten you were

that cold spring day, searching
for guardian ravens at the Tower

and listening to the guide's tales
of beer-drinking zebras and a white

bear let out on a long leash at dawn
to fish in the Thames. How keen

you were to visit the room where the two
young princes died at the hand

of an uncle. To tour the torture chambers.
To keep an eye out for ghosts.

Later, when the cheery Beefeaters
scanned the crowd for a mark,

and spotted you, hiding
behind your father's trench coat,

a scowl on your face,
always hungry, always

wanting something, they knew right
away you were the perfect foil.

Her Paris

Everything changed after
her diagnosis, her favorite city
now a place she travels to
only in her mind while she waits
for something medical — a test,
a consult, a treatment, legs
flopped over the edge of the bed,
hands patiently picking random
pieces of lint from her loose pants,
like leftover bits of the *pain*
au chocolat she would gorge on
each morning before heading out
to explore a new *quartier*.

When the orderly pushes her
down hallways that all look
the same, she closes her eyes.
Three more sets of doors before
it is her stop. She has studied
the map. She knows where
transit lines cross. She knows
the times when she will have to stand,
squeezed against others in the heat,
the smell of so many bodies
commingling, even the French
joke they could bottle,
but not sell, "*Eau de Métro*."

Lying on the pre-op stretcher,
she almost feels at home,
grateful for small comforts,
a plastic blanket pumped full
of warm air hugging her.

Her nose recognizes dust, blood,
urine, what passes for food
from the cafeteria, medical odours
mixed with coffee and the odd whiff
of secondhand smoke. She misses
her pungent *fromagerie* and the
fragrant draw of her *boulangerie* but
after all, here she is just a tourist.

Dead or Alive

You don't disappear. You reappear dead.
— Ed Dorn

At the wheel — driving on the wrong side of the road.
In my bath — bubbles out of nowhere.
In the garden — a bull thistle crowding out the blue iris.

You listen in on every idle conversation,
text me in the night in dreams too sensible to be real.
Where can I go without you?

My grocery cart contains items only you liked.
The clock radio comes on when you had to get up.
You still don't replace the toilet paper roll.

I found a rogue sock in the dryer.
The dog waits for the slam of your car door.
The kid next door asked when you get back from vacation.

I am tired of seeing you everywhere
out of the corner of my eye, of hearing the endless
drone of your voice, lone mosquito in the dark.

Why haven't you left yet? This is not the Old West
with yellowed posters peppered with bullet holes.
Trust me. The reward for your capture expired long ago.

Black Dog Syndrome

These are not the legendary ghost dogs
of night prowling the roadways
and back lanes to scare you
to death with their bad breath
and blazing red eyes.

They are not named Shag or Strike
or Padfoot, have not yet bitten
snarled or growled or given
up hope for a human hand
to stroke their back

or rub their ears, the dream
still alive of a half-full
water dish and a favorite bed.
You can see the longing in their eyes,
in the photos the workers take

to show there is still time,
like a second marriage,
to get it right. Pick me. Love me. Me.
Tails wag, bob and wave
in the shelter's fetid air.

And, like a good matchmaker, decisions
are made. These six will be shipped
to another part of the continent
where black fur is not so feared.
The others will remain here

for an undetermined time, to serve
as backdrops for all the lighter
coloured animals. For the cream, tawny,
buff, spotted, red, yellow, brown,
and white, especially

the white, be their coats long, short,
wiry or curly, whose lucky lives,
on the other side of the chain-link fence,
appear, through the accident of
genetics, cruelly assured.

The Snake Handler's Word of God

Mark 16: 17--18

And these signs will follow those who believe
who crowd themselves into tiny mountain churches all over
Appalachia, in Scrabble Creek and La Follette and Bluefield &
in my Name they will cast out demons, so ready are they
to share the joy of working for the Lord, their hands
covered with old fang bites, scarred and swollen, the law be damned
they will speak with new tongues, their holiness rolling
over the heads of the congregation, thunder in the heat
of vowels and syllables fluid as the speech of spirits &
they will take up serpents, their holy cargo of copperheads
timber rattlers, cottonmouths, jammed into wooden boxes
then released to twist and curl, hand to hand
and if they drink anything deadly like strychnine
from a Mason jar, God's power over poison will surely prevail
and they will be saved, for His Great Love, it will not fail &
it will by no means hurt them, any more than flames
from Coke bottles with oil-soaked wicks held to
skin, soft, young, coarse or old, will burn
signs into true believers in the Holy Ghost, for
they will lay their hands on the sick, in these clandestine
healings, in this revival of charisma, faith mushrooming, like
father like son, preachers who travel to take on the devil
and they will recover, if it isn't their time, in some simple hall
somewhere far from medical help, struggling to breathe,
to move, but mouthing, always, some holy word of God.

Wilf Perreault's *Guiding Light (2002)* as Sanctuary

Everything in this world is like a dream.
The back lane empty in the final hour

between day and night, the last rays
of a late winter sun playing up

a darkening sky, the birds,
if there are birds, nestling in silence

in the dense branches of fir trees,
the other trees bare, no other animals in sight,

no sign of human life apart
from tire tracks in snow that pitted

and melted during the heat of the day,
a large puddle, now stretched across

the alley, mirrors the afterglow, and
the inky lines of telephone wires,

and poles, leading the eye straight
to what otherwise might have been missed

in this shadowy blue landscape,
the faint spires of a church,

the heart of everything in this world,
where light from an open garage

yawns across the lane and the glow
from kitchen windows waves you in,

like a blessing said before meals,
and prayers before bed, in homes

where sheets smell like the sun,
and you can forget the troubles of the day

when you lock the door against
the coming night.

The Heist

Somewhere in Ireland, a thief hoards the heart
of Dublin's patron saint. Maybe he thought
something holy could help his situation

as he pried open the iron cage high on the chapel
wall where the famous relic had been housed
for centuries in a simple wooden box.

But truthfully who would want a wizened
bit of flesh that once pumped blood
through the thin body of a man

who wore a hair shirt, never ate
meat, and fasted one day each week
on bread and water? What wish

could be so great, what dream so
desperately desired? Perhaps the police
have it all wrong. Perhaps this loss is

in fact another miracle, the final one
St. Laurence will perform, a gathering
not of the hungry, the poor

but of what he left on earth —
his skull, his thigh bones — and now,
the very engine behind all his good deeds,

stockpiled near his former monastery
in that dark cave between a rock and a deep lake
where he used to retreat, to pray

in solitude for his too-worldly flock,
emerging now from those long private talks
with his heavenly father, bathed

in light, smiling, feeling at peace
with himself and the world,
and whole again.

How You Reach the Sea

i

Follow the road to the edge of the field.
Take the path down to where
everything that was is still possible.

ii

When there is nothing on the horizon
nothing on the shore, nothing around you,
there will be everything to see.

iii

Go look now. Come back
only when you can say what it is you have seen,
what you know any traveller would want

from such a view, a vision
so simple a child would know
it has to be true.

Acknowledgements

Some of these poems appeared in the following periodicals and anthologies, sometimes in slightly different versions: "My Sicily" appeared under the title of "Mia Sicilia" in Descant Summer 2011 ; "Village Laundry" was published in the 2011 Montreal International Poetry Prize Longlist Anthology (Véhicule Press) and was shortlisted in the 2010 Bridport International Poetry Competition; "Wild Horses" was longlisted in the 2010 Fish International Poetry competition; "Mitterand's Last Meal" placed on the Highly Commended Shortlist of the 2012 Gregory O'Donaghue International Poetry Prize and was published in the Irish journal, *Southword;* "The Snakehandler's Word of God" was longlisted in the 2013 Fish International Poetry competition; "The Woman Who Swallowed History," was included in the 2013 Montreal International Poetry Prize Longlist; "Up At Night" was longlisted in the 2014 Fish International Poetry Competition; and "Wilf Perreault's "*Guiding Light, 2002*" as Sanctuary" appeared in *Wilf Perreault: Up My Alley*, Coteau Books, 2014.

The four Cathedral Village poems were part of a longer group performance piece written and presented by members of the Poets Combine at the 2011 and 2012 Cathedral Village Arts Festivals.

I borrowed a line from Sarah Hannah's poem, "Self-Portrait in a Cocked Hat," for the title and first lines of "The Coat is a River."

The section titles in "Hen House" are the titles of watercolours by Scottish artist Janice Gray RSW.

Agnes Martin's paintings, writings, and life story inspired the poems in "Homage to Happiness." Her abstract minimalist paintings evoke powerful emotions in me.

Harold Rhenisch, my editor, read this manuscript with a careful eye and a sensitive ear, providing stellar support and guidance. I especially appreciated his enthusiasm, energy and willingness to play with multiple versions of many of the poems.

I also want to thank the members of my writing group, The Poets Combine, for their fellowship and ongoing editorial responses to my work — Byrna Barclay, Bob Currie, Katherine Lawrence, Jim McLean, Bruce Rice and Paul Wilson.

Finally, I am grateful for my family's love and encouragement, and their patient acceptance of the many hours of solitude I require in order to write.

DON HALL

Judith Krause is the author of four previous books of poetry, of which the most recent is *Mongrel Love* (Hagios Press, 2008) and a collaborative chapbook, *blue transport/ the insistence of green* (JackPine Press, 2007). Her poems have appeared in Canadian magazines and anthologies and have been published in the USA and Ireland. Awards and honours include the City of Regina Writing Award (1988 and 1998); the Ralph Gustaphson Poetry Award (2006); and residencies and fellowships in the US at the Atlantic Center for the Arts, the Vermont Studio Center, and the Virginia Center for the Creative Arts.

Born and raised in Regina, Judith works as an adult educator, writer, and editor. She has studied writing in Canada, France, and the US, where she completed an MFA in Creative Writing at Warren Wilson College in North Carolina. An active member of the Regina writing community, she has served on boards, judged contests, mentored other writers, taught creative writing classes, and edited periodicals, anthologies, and individual poetry collections. Judith is a founding member of one of Saskatchewan's longest-running writing groups, The Poets Combine.

In 2014, she accepted a two-year term as Saskatchewan's fifth Poet Laureate.